Contents

JELL-O Molds   4

Pies   8

Cakes & Cookies   17

Layered Desserts & Trifles   22

Salads   28

Frozen Delights   31

Entertaining Favorites   35

Seasonal Desserts   39

JELL-O Magic Mousse

"Layers Magically Separate During Refrigeration"

Makes 10 servings, about ½ cup each.

Total: 8 hours 10 minutes (includes refrigerating)

3 cups boiling water
1 package (8-serving size) **JELL-O** Cherry or Lime Flavor Gelatin
1 tub (16 ounces) **COOL WHIP** Whipped Topping, thawed (**COOL WHIP** 16-ounce tub mold can be found in the freezer aisle for a limited time only)

STIR boiling water into dry gelatin mix in medium bowl at least 2 minutes until completely dissolved. Add whipped topping to hot gelatin; stir with wire whisk until whipped topping is completely melted and mixture is well blended. (Mixture will still be thin.)

WASH whipped topping tub mold; dry well. Spray with cooking spray. Fill with gelatin mixture.

REFRIGERATE at least 8 hours or overnight. To unmold, dip tub into warm water 15 seconds. Unmold onto serving plate just before serving. Store leftover dessert in refrigerator.

Chocolate Drizzle Garnish: Melt 1 square **BAKER'S** Semi-Sweet Baking Chocolate in microwaveable bowl on HIGH 1 minute; stir until melted. Cool slightly. Pour into resealable plastic bag. Snip off small piece from one of the bottom corners of bag; squeeze chocolate over serving plate as desired. Refrigerate until firm. Unmold dessert onto prepared plate just before serving.

Chocolate-Covered Cherries: Pat maraschino cherries dry with paper towels; set aside. Microwave 2 squares **BAKER'S** Semi-Sweet Baking Chocolate in microwaveable bowl on HIGH 1 minute; stir until melted. Dip cherries in chocolate; place on wax paper-covered baking sheet. Refrigerate until firm.

Refreshing Double-Melon Delight

Makes 10 servings.

Total: 4 hours 40 minutes (includes refrigerating)

2   cups boiling water
1   package (8-serving size) **JELL-O** Lemon Flavor Gelatin
    Ice cubes
1   cup cold water
2   cups honeydew melon balls
2   cups cantaloupe balls
6   small mint leaves

STIR boiling water into dry gelatin mix in large bowl at least 2 minutes until completely dissolved. Add enough ice to cold water to measure 1½ cups. Add to gelatin; stir. Remove any undissolved ice. Refrigerate 30 minutes or until slightly thickened (consistency of unbeaten egg whites).

STIR in melon balls and mint leaves. Spoon into 9×5-inch loaf pan.

REFRIGERATE 4 hours or until firm. Unmold. Store leftover gelatin in refrigerator.

Jazz It Up: Not a mint lover? Simply omit mint leaves.

15 Minute Prep

Mandarin Mousse Mold

Makes 12 servings, ½ cup each.

Total: 4 hours 45 minutes

1½ cups boiling water

1 package (8-serving size) or 2 packages (4-serving size each) **JELL-O** Orange Flavor Gelatin

1 cup cold water

1 can (11 ounces) mandarin orange segments, drained

1 tub (8 ounces) **COOL WHIP** Whipped Topping, thawed, divided

STIR boiling water into gelatin in large bowl 2 minutes until completely dissolved. Stir in cold water. Place orange segments in 6-cup mold; spoon 2 cups gelatin mixture into mold over oranges. Refrigerate about 30 minutes or until set, but not firm (should stick to finger).

MEANWHILE, refrigerate remaining gelatin mixture about 30 minutes or until slightly thickened (consistency of unbeaten egg whites). Stir in 2 cups of the whipped topping with wire whisk until well blended. Pour over gelatin layer in mold.

REFRIGERATE 4 hours or until firm. Unmold. Serve with remaining whipped topping. Store leftover gelatin mold in refrigerator.

Healthy Living: Save 1 gram fat per serving by using **COOL WHIP LITE** Whipped Topping.

Fresh Fruit Parfait Mold

Makes 6 cups.

Total: 5 hours 45 minutes

1½ cups boiling water
1 package (8-serving size) **JELL-O** Strawberry Flavor Sugar Free Low Calorie Gelatin
1½ cups cold water
¾ cup blueberries
¾ cup chopped strawberries
1½ cups thawed **COOL WHIP LITE** Whipped Topping

STIR boiling water into gelatin in large bowl at least 2 minutes until completely dissolved. Stir in cold water. Refrigerate about 1¼ hours or until slightly thickened (consistency of unbeaten egg whites). Reserve 1½ cups of the gelatin at room temperature.

STIR fruit into remaining gelatin. Spoon into 6-cup mold sprayed with cooking spray. Refrigerate 15 minutes or until set but not firm (should stick to finger when touched and should mound).

STIR whipped topping into reserved gelatin with wire whisk until smooth. Spoon over gelatin in mold.

Refrigerate 4 hours or until firm. Unmold. Store leftover dessert in refrigerator.

Substitute: Substitute 2 packages (4-serving size each) strawberry gelatin for 1 package (8 ounces) gelatin.

15 Minute Prep

Triple Layer Eggnog Pie

Makes 10 servings, 1 slice each.

Total: 3 hours 15 minutes (includes refrigerating)

10 **KRAFT** Caramels
 1 cup cold milk, divided
 1 **HONEY MAID** Graham Pie Crust (6 ounces)
 ½ cup **PLANTERS** Chopped Pecans, toasted
 1 cup cold eggnog
 2 packages (4-serving size each) **JELL-O** Vanilla Flavor Instant Pudding & Pie Filling
 1 tub (8 ounces) **COOL WHIP** Whipped Topping, thawed, divided

PLACE caramels and 1 tablespoon of the milk in microwaveable bowl. Microwave on MEDIUM (50%) 30 seconds or until caramels are completely melted when stirred. Pour into crust; sprinkle with pecans.

POUR remaining milk and eggnog into large bowl. Add dry pudding mixes. Beat with wire whisk 2 minutes or until well blended. (Mixture will be thick.) Spoon 1½ cups of the pudding over pecans in crust.

ADD half of the whipped topping to remaining pudding; stir until well blended. Spread over pudding layer in crust; top with remaining whipped topping. Refrigerate at least 3 hours before serving. Store leftover pie in refrigerator.

Jazz It Up: Sprinkle pie with ground nutmeg or ground cinnamon just before serving.

COOL 'N EASY Pie

Makes 8 servings, 1 slice each.

Total: 4 hours 30 minutes (includes refrigeration)

⅔ cup boiling water

1 package (4-serving size) **JELL-O** Strawberry Flavor Gelatin

Ice cubes

½ cup cold water

1 tub (8 ounces) **COOL WHIP** Whipped Topping, thawed

1 **HONEY MAID** Graham Pie Crust (6 ounces)

STIR boiling water into dry gelatin mix in large bowl at least 2 minutes until completely dissolved. Add enough ice to cold water to measure 1 cup. Add to gelatin; stir until slightly thickened. Remove any unmelted ice. Add whipped topping; stir with wire whisk until well blended. Refrigerate 15 to 20 minutes or until mixture is thick enough to mound.

SPOON into crust.

REFRIGERATE at least 4 hours or overnight until firm. Store leftover pie in refrigerator.

Healthy Living: Save 30 calories, 4g of total fat and 2g of saturated fat per serving by preparing with **COOL WHIP LITE** Whipped Topping and a reduced-fat graham cracker crust.

Pies

9

OREO Ice Cream Shop Pie

Makes 10 servings, 1 slice each.

Total: 4 hours 15 minutes (includes freezing)

- ½ cup hot fudge dessert topping, divided
- 1 **OREO** Pie Crust (6 ounces)
- 1 tub (8 ounces) **COOL WHIP** Whipped Topping, thawed, divided
- 1¼ cups cold milk
- 2 packages (4-serving size each) **JELL-O OREO** Flavor Instant Pudding & Pie Filling

REMOVE 2 tablespoons of the fudge topping; set aside. Spoon remaining topping into crust; spread to evenly cover bottom of crust. Top with half of the whipped topping; freeze 10 minutes.

POUR milk into large bowl. Add dry pudding mixes. Beat with wire whisk 2 minutes or until well blended. (Mixture will be thick.) Gently stir in remaining whipped topping. Spoon over whipped topping layer in crust.

FREEZE 4 hours or until firm. Remove pie from freezer 15 minutes before serving. Let stand at room temperature to soften slightly. Drizzle with the reserved 2 tablespoons fudge topping. Store leftover pie in freezer.

Substitute: For more chocolate flavor, prepare as directed using an **HONEY MAID** Graham Pie Crust.

Pies
10

Lime Chiffon Pie

Makes 8 servings, 1 slice each.

Total: 4 hours 30 minutes (includes refrigerating)

⅔ cup boiling water

1 package (4-serving size) **JELL-O** Lime Flavor Sugar Free Low Calorie Gelatin

Ice cubes

½ cup cold water

1½ teaspoons grated lime peel

2 tablespoons lime juice

2 cups thawed **COOL WHIP FREE** Whipped Topping

1 ready-to-use reduced fat graham cracker crumb crust (6 ounces)

STIR boiling water into dry gelatin mix in large bowl at least 2 minutes until completely dissolved. Add enough ice to cold water to measure 1 cup. Add to gelatin; stir until ice is completely melted. Stir in lime peel and juice.

ADD whipped topping; stir with wire whisk until well blended. Refrigerate 15 to 20 minutes or until mixture is very thick and will mound. Spoon into crust.

REFRIGERATE at least 4 hours or overnight. Store leftover pie in refrigerator.

Lemon Chiffon Pie: Prepare as directed, using **JELL-O** Lemon Flavor Sugar Free Low Calorie Gelatin, lemon peel and lemon juice.

Fresh Raspberry-Lemon Pie

Makes 8 servings, 1 slice each.

Total: 4 hours 15 minutes (includes refrigeration)

1 package (8 ounces) **PHILADELPHIA** Cream Cheese, softened
1 cup cold milk
1 package (4-serving size) **JELL-O** Lemon Flavor Instant Pudding & Pie Filling
2 teaspoons grated lemon peel
2 cups thawed **COOL WHIP** Whipped Topping, divided
1 **HONEY MAID** Graham Pie Crust (6 ounces)
1 cup raspberries

BEAT cream cheese, milk, dry pudding mix and lemon peel in large bowl with wire whisk until well blended. Gently stir in 1 cup of the whipped topping.

SPOON into crust; top with remaining 1 cup whipped topping.

REFRIGERATE 4 hours or until firm. Top with raspberries just before serving. Store leftover pie in refrigerator.

Size-Wise: Save room for this special-occasion dessert by planning ahead. For example, watch portions and choose lower-fat foods beforehand.

Double Layer Pumpkin Pie

Makes 10 servings, 1 slice each.

Total: 4 hours 20 minutes (includes refrigerating)

4 ounces (½ of 8-ounce package) **PHILADELPHIA** Cream Cheese, softened
1 tablespoon milk
1 tablespoon sugar
1 tub (8 ounces) **COOL WHIP** Whipped Topping, thawed, divided
1 **HONEY MAID** Graham Pie Crust (6 ounces)
1 cup milk
1 can (15 ounces) pumpkin
2 packages (4-serving size each) **JELL-O** Vanilla Flavor Instant Pudding & Pie Filling
1 teaspoon ground cinnamon
½ teaspoon ground ginger
¼ teaspoon ground cloves

MIX cream cheese, 1 tablespoon milk and the sugar in large bowl with wire whisk until well blended. Gently stir in half of the whipped topping. Spread into bottom of crust.

POUR 1 cup milk into large bowl. Add pumpkin, dry pudding mixes and spices. Beat with wire whisk 2 minutes or until well blended. (Mixture will be thick.) Spread over cream cheese layer.

REFRIGERATE 4 hours or until set. Top with remaining whipped topping just before serving. Store leftover pie in refrigerator.

Double Layer Pecan Pumpkin Pie: Prepare as directed, stirring in ¼ cup chopped toasted **PLANTERS** Pecans along with the whipped topping.

15 Minute Prep

Holiday Mix & Match Pudding Pie

Makes 10 servings, 1 slice each.

Take 2 cups cold milk, 2 packages (4-serving size each) or 1 package (8-serving size) **JELL-O** Chocolate or Vanilla Flavor Instant Pudding & Pie Filling and 1 tub (8 ounces) thawed **COOL WHIP** Whipped Topping and mix & match your recipe from these options...

recipe options	**crust** and **filling** choices	**special extra** possibilities
Peppermint-Chocolate	**HONEY MAID** Graham Pie Crust; 1 cup **JET-PUFFED** Miniature Marshmallows	10 peppermint candies, coarsely chopped; wedges of Peppermint Bark
Raspberry-Double Chocolate	**OREO** Pie Crust; 1 cup fresh raspberries	20 fresh raspberries; White Chocolate Curls; 2 teaspoons powdered sugar
Black Forest	**OREO** Pie Crust; 10 **OREO** Chocolate Sandwich Cookies, quartered	1 cup cherry pie filling; drizzle with 1 square melted **BAKER'S** Semi-Sweet Baking Chocolate
Banana-Caramel Chocolate	**OREO** Pie Crust; 1 cup sliced bananas	13 Chocolate-Dipped Pecans; 5 **KRAFT** Caramels melted with 1 teaspoon milk

Then follow our simple steps:

1. **POUR** milk into medium bowl. Add dry pudding mixes. Beat with wire whisk 2 minutes or until well blended. (Mixture will be thick.)

2. **SPOON** 1½ cups of the pudding into 1 (16-ounce) **crust**; top with **filling**. Gently stir 1½ cups of the whipped topping into remaining pudding; spoon over pie.

3. **REFRIGERATE** 3 hours. Cover with remaining 1½ cups whipped topping just before serving. Top with **special extras.** Store leftover pie in refrigerator.

Peppermint Bark: Microwave 4 squares **BAKER'S** Semi-Sweet Baking Chocolate in microwaveable bowl on HIGH 1½ to 2 minutes or until melted, stirring every 30 seconds. Stir in ¼ cup crushed peppermint candies (about 10 candies). Spread thinly onto wax paper-lined baking sheet; refrigerate until firm. Break into pieces; place on top of pie.

White Chocolate Curls: Microwave 1 square **BAKER'S** Premium White Baking Chocolate on HIGH 15 seconds. Slowly pull a vegetable peeler along one side of the chocolate square to create a curl. Use wooden pick to arrange curls in center of pie.

Chocolate-Dipped Pecans: Microwave 1 square **BAKER'S** Semi-Sweet Baking Chocolate in microwaveable bowl on HIGH 30 seconds or until melted; stir. Dip one end of each pecan half in chocolate. Place on wax paper-lined baking sheet; refrigerate until firm. Arrange over pie.

15 Minute Prep

Decadent Triple Layer Mud Pie

Makes 10 servings, 1 slice each.

Total: 3 hours 25 minutes (includes refrigerating)

- 3 squares **BAKER'S** Semi-Sweet Baking Chocolate, melted
- ¼ cup canned sweetened condensed milk
- 1 **OREO** Pie Crust (6 ounces)
- ½ cup chopped **PLANTERS** Pecans, toasted
- 2 cups cold milk
- 2 packages (4-serving size each) **JELL-O** Chocolate Flavor Instant Pudding & Pie Filling
- 1 tub (8 ounces) **COOL WHIP** Whipped Topping, thawed, divided

MIX chocolate and condensed milk until well blended. Pour into crust; sprinkle with pecans.

POUR milk into large bowl. Add dry pudding mixes. Beat with wire whisk 2 minutes or until well blended. (Mixture will be thick.) Spoon 1½ cups of the pudding over pecans in crust. Add half of the whipped topping to remaining pudding; stir with wire whisk until well blended. Spread over pudding layer in crust; top with remaining whipped topping.

REFRIGERATE 3 hours. Store leftover pie in refrigerator.

How To Toast Nuts: Preheat oven to 350°F. Spread pecans in single layer in shallow baking pan. Bake 5 to 7 minutes or until lightly toasted, stirring occasionally.

Pies

16

JELL-O "Dive-on-In" Cake

Makes 15 servings, 1 slice each.

Total: 4 hours 15 minutes (includes refrigeration)

- 1 package (2-layer size) yellow cake mix
- 2 cups boiling water
- 2 packages (4-serving size each) **JELL-O** Berry Blue Flavor Gelatin
- 1 cup cold water
- 1 tub (8 ounces) **COOL WHIP** Whipped Topping, thawed
- 56 Mini **OREO** Bite Size Chocolate Sandwich Cookies
- 6 **TEDDY GRAHAMS** Graham Snacks
- 5 ring-shaped chewy fruit snacks
- 4 bite-size fish-shaped chewy fruit snacks
- 1 small rectangular **HONEY MAID** Honey Graham

PREPARE and bake cake mix in 13×9-inch baking pan as directed on package. Cool completely. Invert cake onto large platter; remove pan. Using a serrated knife, cut and scoop out a shallow rectangle from center of cake, leaving a 2-inch border of cake on all sides and a thin layer of cake on the bottom. Reserve removed cake for snacking or other use.

STIR boiling water into dry gelatin mix in large bowl at least 2 minutes until completely dissolved. Stir in cold water. Refrigerate 1¼ hours or until slightly thickened (consistency of unbeaten egg whites). (Or, see Shortcut.) Pour thickened gelatin into center of cake. Refrigerate 3 hours or until set.

FROST borders of cake with whipped topping. Decorate with remaining ingredients as desired to resemble a swimming pool. Store leftover cake in refrigerator.

Shortcut: For a quick-set gelatin, simply add 4 cups ice cubes to the dissolved gelatin mixture in place of the 1 cup cold water; stir 8 minutes or until gelatin begins to thicken (spoon drawn through leaves a definite impression). Remove any unmelted ice. Pour thickened gelatin into center of cake; continue as directed.

Angel Lush

Makes 10 servings, 1 slice each.

Total: 1 hour 15 minutes (includes refrigeration)

- 1 can (20 ounces) crushed pineapple in juice, undrained
- 1 package (4-serving size) **JELL-O** Vanilla Flavor Fat Free Sugar Free Instant Reduced Calorie Pudding & Pie Filling
- 1 cup thawed **COOL WHIP LITE** Whipped Topping
- 1 package (10 ounces) round angel food cake
- 10 fresh strawberries

MIX pineapple with its juice and the dry pudding mix in medium bowl. Gently stir in whipped topping.

CUT cake horizontally into 3 layers. Place bottom cake layer, cut-side up, on serving plate; top with 1⅓ cups of the pudding mixture. Cover with middle cake layer and an additional 1 cup of the remaining pudding mixture. Top with remaining cake layer; spread top of dessert with the remaining pudding mixture.

REFRIGERATE at least 1 hour. Top with strawberries just before serving. Store leftover dessert in refrigerator.

How To Cut Angel Food Cake: Use a serrated knife and gentle sawing motion to easily cut the angel food cake.

Substitute: Prepare as directed, using **COOL WHIP** Sugar Free Whipped Topping.

Chocolate-Candy Cane Cake

Makes 18 servings, 1 slice each.

Total: 1 hour 40 minutes (includes cooling)

1 package (2-layer size) chocolate cake mix
1 package (4-serving size) **JELL-O** Chocolate Flavor Instant Pudding & Pie Filling
4 eggs
1 container (8 ounces) **BREAKSTONE'S** or **KNUDSEN** Sour Cream
½ cup vegetable oil
½ cup water
4 squares **BAKER'S** Semi-Sweet Baking Chocolate, chopped
18 small candy canes, coarsely crushed (about 1 cup), divided
1 tub (8 ounces) **COOL WHIP** Whipped Topping, thawed

PREHEAT oven to 350°F. Lightly grease 2 (9-inch) round cake pans. Beat cake mix, dry pudding mix, eggs, sour cream, oil and water in large bowl with electric mixer on low speed just until moistened, stopping frequently to scrape side of bowl. Beat on medium speed 2 minutes or until well blended. Stir in chopped chocolate and 2 tablespoons of the crushed candy canes. Spoon evenly into prepared pans.

BAKE 35 to 40 minutes or until toothpick inserted in centers comes out clean. Cool 10 minutes. Loosen cakes from sides of pans with metal spatula or knife. Invert cakes onto wire racks; carefully remove pans. Cool completely.

PLACE 1 of the cake layers on serving plate; spread evenly with 1 cup of the whipped topping. Top with remaining cake layer. Frost top and side of cake with remaining whipped topping. Sprinkle with remaining crushed candy canes just before serving. Store leftover cake in refrigerator.

Substitute: Melt 1 additional square **BAKER'S** Semi-Sweet Baking Chocolate; cool. Drizzle over cake just before serving. Then, garnish with raspberries.

Lovin' Sweetcakes

Makes 24 servings, 1 cupcake each.

Total: 1 hour

- 1 package (2-layer size) white cake mix
- 1 package (4-serving size) **JELL-O** Strawberry Flavor Gelatin, or any red flavor
- 1 tub (8 ounces) **COOL WHIP** Whipped Topping, thawed
- ¼ cup seasonal colored sprinkles

PREPARE cake batter as directed on package. Stir in dry powdered gelatin until well blended.

LINE 24 medium muffin cups with paper liners. Pour batter evenly into cups, filling each cup ½ full. Bake as directed on package for cupcakes. Cool completely.

SPREAD 2 tablespoons whipped topping onto top of each cupcake. Decorate each with ¼ teaspoon sprinkles as desired. Store cupcakes in refrigerator.

Fun Idea: Use Valentine's Day cupcake liners for a special look.

Tip: For heart-shaped cupcakes, place a small marble or ½-inch ball of foil between each liner and one side of the cup, pushing the paper in to form a heart shape. Bake as directed on package for cupcakes. Cool completely; remove marble or foil.

Cakes & Cookies

20

JELL-O Pastel Cookies

Makes about 5 dozen cookies or 30 servings, 2 cookies each.

Total: 40 minutes

- 3½ cups flour
- 1 teaspoon **CALUMET** Baking Powder
- 1½ cups (3 sticks) butter or margarine, softened
- 1 cup sugar
- 2 packages (4-serving size each) **JELL-O** Gelatin, any flavor, divided
- 1 egg
- 1 teaspoon vanilla

PREHEAT oven to 400°F. Mix flour and baking powder; set aside. Beat butter in large bowl with electric mixer on medium speed until creamy. Gradually add sugar and 1 package of the dry gelatin, beating until light and fluffy. Add egg and vanilla; mix well. Gradually add flour mixture, beating until well blended after each addition.

SHAPE dough into 1-inch balls. Place, 2 inches apart, on ungreased baking sheets. Flatten with bottom of clean glass. Sprinkle with remaining dry gelatin.

BAKE 8 to 10 minutes or until edges are lightly browned. Remove from baking sheets to wire racks. Cool completely. Store in tightly covered container at room temperature.

Make Ahead: To freeze, place balls of uncooked dough on wax paper-covered baking sheet; freeze until firm. Transfer to resealable freezer-weight plastic bag; freeze up to 3 months. Thaw on baking sheets before baking.

Floating Fruit Parfaits

Makes 6 servings.

Total: 1 hour 35 minutes (includes refrigeration)

½ cup sliced strawberries
¾ cup boiling water
1 package (4-serving size) **JELL-O** Strawberry Flavor Sugar Free Low Calorie Gelatin
½ cup cold water
¾ cup ice cubes
1 cup plus 6 tablespoons thawed **COOL WHIP LITE** Whipped Topping, divided

SPOON strawberries evenly into 6 parfait or dessert glasses. Stir boiling water into dry gelatin mix in medium bowl at least 2 minutes until completely dissolved. Add cold water and ice cubes; stir until ice is completely melted. Remove ¾ cup of the gelatin; pour evenly over strawberries in glasses. Refrigerate 20 minutes or until gelatin is set but not firm.

ADD 1 cup of the whipped topping to remaining gelatin in bowl; stir with wire whisk until well blended. Spoon evenly over gelatin in glasses.

REFRIGERATE 1 hour or until firm. Top each parfait with 1 tablespoon of the remaining whipped topping just before serving. Store leftover parfaits in refrigerator.

Variation: Prepare as directed, using **JELL-O** Orange Flavor Sugar Free Low Calorie Gelatin and substituting cantaloupe balls for the strawberries.

Nutrition Bonus: Satisfy your sweet tooth with this elegant low-fat dessert. As a bonus, the strawberries provide a good source of vitamin C!

Substitute: Prepare as directed, using **COOL WHIP** Sugar Free Whipped Topping.

Strawberry Pretzel Squares

Makes 20 servings, I square each.

Total: 4 hours 55 minutes (incudes refrigerating)

2 cups finely crushed pretzels
½ cup sugar, divided
⅔ cup butter or margarine, melted
12 ounces (1½ [8-ounce] packages) **PHILADELPHIA** Cream Cheese, softened
2 tablespoons milk
I cup thawed **COOL WHIP** Whipped Topping
2 cups boiling water
I package (8-serving size) **JELL-O** Strawberry Flavor Gelatin
1½ cups cold water
I quart (4 cups) strawberries, sliced

PREHEAT oven to 350°F. Mix pretzels, ¼ cup of the sugar and the butter. Press firmly onto bottom of 13×9-inch baking pan. Bake 10 minutes. Cool.

BEAT cream cheese, remaining ¼ cup sugar and milk until well blended. Gently stir in whipped topping. Spread over crust. Refrigerate until ready to use.

MEANWHILE, stir boiling water into gelatin in large bowl at least 2 minutes until completely dissolved. Stir in cold water. Refrigerate 1½ hours or until thickened (spoon drawn through leaves definite impression). Stir in strawberries. Spoon over cream cheese layer. Refrigerate 3 hours or until firm. Cut into 20 squares to serve. Store leftover dessert in refrigerator.

Make It Easy: Substitute I package (20 ounces) frozen whole strawberries, sliced, for the fresh strawberries. Stir into gelatin along with the cold water. Refrigerate 10 to 15 minutes or until thickened, then spoon over cream cheese layer. Continue as directed.

Layered Desserts & Trifles

Chocolate-Mint Parfait

Makes 6 servings, 1 parfait each.

Total: 30 minutes (includes refrigerating)

2   cups cold milk
1/4 teaspoon peppermint extract
1   package (4-serving size) **JELL-O** Chocolate Flavor Instant Pudding & Pie Filling
6   drops green food coloring
1   cup thawed **COOL WHIP** Whipped Topping
    Additional **COOL WHIP** Whipped Topping (optional)

POUR milk and peppermint extract into medium bowl. Add dry pudding mix. Beat with wire whisk 2 minutes or until well blended; set aside.

ADD food coloring to the 1 cup whipped topping; stir gently until well blended. Layer pudding and whipped topping alternately in 6 parfait glasses.

REFRIGERATE at least 15 minutes before serving. Top with additional whipped topping, if desired.

Substitute: Substitute 1/4 teaspoon almond extract or 1/2 teaspoon ground cinnamon for the mint extract to customize the flavor of these parfaits.

Chocolate Passion Bowl

Makes 16 servings, about ⅔ cup each.

Total: 1 hour 20 minutes (includes refrigerating)

3   cups cold milk
2   packages (4-serving size each) **JELL-O** Chocolate Flavor Instant Pudding & Pie Filling
1   tub (8 ounces) **COOL WHIP** French Vanilla Whipped Topping, thawed, divided
1   baked (9-inch-square) brownie layer, cooled, cut into 1-inch cubes (about 5½ cups)
1   pint (2 cups) raspberries

POUR milk into large bowl. Add dry pudding mixes. Beat with wire whisk 2 minutes or until well blended. Gently stir in 1 cup of the whipped topping.

PLACE half of the brownie cubes in 2-quart serving bowl; top with half each of the pudding mixture, raspberries and the remaining whipped topping. Repeat all layers.

REFRIGERATE at least 1 hour or until ready to serve. Store leftover dessert in refrigerator.

Jazz It Up: Chop 2 chocolate-coated caramel-peanut nougat bars (2.07 ounces each). Assemble dessert as directed, topping each layer of raspberries with layer of half of the chopped nougat bars.

**Layered
Desserts &
Trifles**

25

Easy Southern Banana Pudding

Makes 14 servings, about ⅔ cup each.

Total: 3 hours 20 minutes (includes refrigeration)

- 3 cups cold milk
- 2 packages (4-serving size each) **JELL-O** Vanilla Flavor Instant Pudding & Pie Filling
- 30 **NILLA** Wafers
- 3 medium bananas, sliced
- 1 tub (8 ounces) **COOL WHIP** Whipped Topping, thawed

POUR milk into large bowl. Add dry pudding mixes. Beat with wire whisk 2 minutes or until well blended. Let stand 5 minutes.

ARRANGE half of the wafers on bottom and up side of 2-quart serving bowl; top with layers of half each of the banana slices and pudding. Repeat all layers. Cover with whipped topping.

REFRIGERATE 3 hours. Store leftover dessert in refrigerator.

Healthy Living: Save 60 calories and 3.5 grams of fat per serving by preparing with fat free milk, **JELL-O** Vanilla Flavor Fat Free Sugar Free Instant Reduced Calorie Pudding & Pie Filling, Reduced Fat **NILLA** Wafers and **COOL WHIP LITE** Whipped Topping.

Double Chocolate NILLA Squares

Makes 24 servings, 1 square each.

Total: 3 hours 15 minutes (includes refrigerating)

64 **NILLA** Wafers, divided
3 tablespoons sugar
6 tablespoons butter or margarine, softened, divided
4 squares **BAKER'S** Semi-Sweet Baking Chocolate
2½ cups cold milk
2 packages (4-serving size each) **JELL-O** Chocolate Flavor Instant Pudding & Pie Filling
1½ cups (½ of 8-ounce tub) thawed **COOL WHIP** Whipped Topping

CRUSH 40 of the wafers; mix with sugar and 5 tablespoons of the butter until well blended. Press firmly onto bottom of 13×9-inch baking pan to form crust.

PLACE chocolate and remaining 1 tablespoon butter in small microwaveable bowl. Microwave on HIGH 1 minute or until butter is melted. Stir until chocolate is completely melted. Drizzle over crust with spoon.

POUR milk into large bowl. Add pudding mixes. Beat with wire whisk 2 minutes. Gently stir in whipped topping. Spread half of the pudding mixture over crust; top with remaining 24 wafers. Cover with remaining pudding mixture. Refrigerate at least 3 hours. Cut into 24 squares.

Jazz It Up: Garnish each square with an additional halved **NILLA** Wafer drizzled with chocolate.

10 Minute Prep

Festive Cranberry-Pineapple Salad

Makes 14 servings, ½ cup each.

Total: 5 hours 40 minutes (includes refrigerating)

1 can (20 ounces) **DOLE** Crushed Pineapple, undrained
2 packages (4-serving size each) or 1 package (8-serving size) **JELL-O** Raspberry Flavor Gelatin
1 can (16 ounces) whole berry cranberry sauce
1 medium **DOLE** Apple, chopped
⅔ cup chopped **PLANTERS** Walnuts
Apple Slices (optional)

DRAIN pineapple, reserving liquid in 1-quart liquid measuring cup. Add enough cold water to reserved liquid to measure 3 cups; pour into large saucepan. Bring to boil; remove from heat. Add gelatin; stir at least 2 minutes until completely dissolved. Add cranberry sauce; stir until well blended. (Note: Due to the presence of whole berries in the cranberry sauce, the gelatin mixture will not be smooth.) Pour into large bowl. Refrigerate 1½ hours or until slightly thickened (consistency of unbeaten egg whites).

STIR in remaining pineapple, apple and walnuts; stir gently until well blended. Pour into medium serving bowl.

REFRIGERATE 4 hours or until firm. Garnish with apple slices just before serving, if desired. Store leftover gelatin in refrigerator.

Molded Cranberry-Pineapple Salad: To serve as a molded salad, substitute a 6-cup mold for the serving bowl. Also, use 1 can (8¼ ounces) **DOLE** Crushed Pineapple, ⅓ cup chopped **PLANTERS** Walnuts and add enough cold water to the reserved pineapple liquid to measure 2 cups.

Makes 10 servings, ½ cup each.

DOLE is a trademark of Dole Food Company, Inc.

Watergate Salad

Makes 8 servings, about ½ cup each.

Total: 1 hour 15 minutes (includes refrigerating)

1 package (4-serving size) **JELL-O** Pistachio Flavor Instant Pudding & Pie Filling
1 can (20 ounces) **DOLE** Crushed Pineapple, in juice, undrained
1 cup **JET-PUFFED** Miniature Marshmallows
½ cup chopped **PLANTERS** Pecans
1½ cups (½ of 8-ounce tub) thawed **COOL WHIP** Whipped Topping

MIX dry pudding mix, pineapple, marshmallows and pecans in large bowl until well blended.
ADD whipped topping; stir gently until well blended. Cover.
REFRIGERATE 1 hour or until ready to serve.

Jazz It Up: Serve this treat in small individual dessert dishes garnished with a maraschino cherry.

DOLE is a trademark of Dole Food Company, Inc.

10 Minute Prep

Summer Fruit Punch "Salad"

Makes 12 servings, ½ cup each.

Total: 2 hours 10 minutes (includes refrigeration)

- 1 package (4-serving size) **JELL-O** Cherry Flavor Gelatin
- 1 package (4-serving size) **JELL-O** Strawberry Flavor Gelatin
- 1½ cups boiling water
- Ice cubes
- 1 cup orange juice
- 1 pint (2 cups) strawberries, sliced
- 1 cup seedless grape halves
- 1½ cups thawed **COOL WHIP** Strawberry Whipped Topping

COMBINE dry gelatin mixes in large bowl. Stir in boiling water at least 2 minutes until completely dissolved. Add enough ice cubes to orange juice to measure 2¼ cups. Add to gelatin; stir until slightly thickened. Remove any unmelted ice. Stir in fruit.

POUR into large serving bowl.

REFRIGERATE 2 hours or until firm. Top with the whipped topping just before serving. Store leftover dessert in refrigerator.

Substitute: Substitute 2 packages (4-serving size each) **JELL-O** Mixed Fruit Flavor Gelatin for the 1 package each cherry and strawberry gelatins.

Frozen Peach Shortcake Squares

Makes 12 servings, 1 slice each.

Total: 3 hours 10 minutes (includes freezing)

1   tub (8 ounces) **COOL WHIP** Whipped Topping, thawed
1   pint (2 cups) vanilla ice cream, softened
1   package (4-serving size) **JELL-O** Peach Flavor Gelatin
    (unprepared)
4   cups pound cake cubes
¼   cup raspberry preserves
12 small peach slices
12 raspberries

STIR whipped topping, ice cream and dry gelatin in large bowl until well blended. Stir in cake cubes. Spoon into 8-inch square pan.

FREEZE 3 hours or until firm.

DRIZZLE with raspberry preserves. Cut into squares. Top each square with 1 peach slice and 1 raspberry. Store leftover dessert in freezer.

Substitute: Prepare as directed, using **COOL WHIP LITE** Whipped Topping, low-fat ice cream, **JELL-O** Peach Sugar Free Low Calorie Gelatin and reduced fat pound cake.

Low-Fat Raspberry Summer Sensation

Makes 12 servings, 1 slice each.

Total: 3 hours 25 minutes (includes freezing)

- 1 pint (2 cups) raspberry sorbet or sherbet, softened
- 1 cup cold fat free milk
- 1 package (4-serving size) **JELL-O** Vanilla Flavor Fat Free Sugar Free Instant Reduced Calorie Pudding & Pie Filling
- 1 tub (8 ounces) **COOL WHIP FREE** Whipped Topping, thawed
- 1 cup raspberries

LINE 9×5-inch loaf pan with foil. Spoon sorbet into pan; freeze 10 minutes.

POUR milk into large bowl. Add dry pudding mix. Beat with wire whisk 2 minutes or until well blended. Gently stir in whipped topping; spread evenly over sorbet in pan.

FREEZE 3 hours or overnight. To unmold, invert pan onto plate; remove foil. Top evenly with raspberries. Let stand 10 to 15 minutes to soften slightly before cutting into 12 slices to serve. Place 1 slice on each of 12 dessert plates. Store leftover dessert in freezer.

How To Soften Sorbet: Soften sorbet in microwave on MEDIUM (50%) for 10 to 15 seconds or until slightly softened.

JELL-O Homemade Pudding Pops

Makes 6 servings, 1 pop each.

Total: 5 hours 10 minutes (includes freezing)

2 cups cold milk
1 package (4-serving size) **JELL-O** Chocolate Flavor Instant Pudding & Pie Filling

POUR milk into medium bowl. Add dry pudding mix. Beat with wire whisk 2 minutes.

SPOON evenly into 6 (5-ounce) paper or plastic cups. Insert wooden pop stick or plastic spoon into center of each cup for handle.

FREEZE 5 hours or until firm. To remove pops from cups, place bottoms of cups under warm running water for 15 seconds. Press firmly on bottoms of cups to release pops. (Do not twist or pull pop sticks.) Store leftover pops in freezer.

Nutrition Bonus: Kids are sure to love this low-fat frozen treat. As a bonus, the milk provides a good source of calcium.

Rocket Pops

Makes 16 servings, 1 pop each.

Total: 7 hours 30 minutes (includes freezing)

1 package (4-serving size) **JELL-O** Cherry Flavor Gelatin
1 cup sugar, divided
2 cups boiling water, divided
  Ice cubes
2 cups cold water, divided
1 package (4-serving size) **JELL-O** Berry Blue Flavor Gelatin
1 tub (8 ounces) **COOL WHIP** Whipped Topping, thawed

COMBINE dry cherry gelatin mix and ½ cup of the sugar in medium bowl. Add 1 cup of the boiling water; stir at least 2 minutes until gelatin is completely dissolved. Add enough ice cubes to 1 cup of the cold water to measure 2 cups. Add to gelatin; stir until ice is completely melted. Pour evenly into 16 (5-ounce) paper or plastic cups, adding about ¼ cup of the gelatin to each cup. Freeze 1 hour.

MEANWHILE, combine dry blue gelatin mix and remaining ½ cup sugar in medium bowl. Add remaining 1 cup boiling water; stir at least 2 minutes until gelatin is completely dissolved. Add enough ice cubes to remaining 1 cup cold water to measure 2 cups. Add to gelatin; stir until ice is completely melted. Refrigerate 1 hour.

SPOON about 3 tablespoons of the whipped topping over cherry gelatin in each cup; top evenly with blue gelatin, adding about ¼ cup of the gelatin to each cup. Freeze 1 hour or until almost firm. Insert wooden pop stick or plastic spoon into center of each cup for handle. Freeze an additional 4 hours or overnight. To remove pops from cups, place bottoms of cups under warm running water for 15 seconds. Press firmly on bottoms of cups to release pops. (Do not twist or pull pop sticks.) Store leftover pops in freezer.

Note: Wooden popsicle sticks can be found at craft stores.

Low-Fat Tropical Dream Cheesecake

Makes 8 servings, 1 slice each.

Total: 4 hours 15 minutes

1 **HONEY MAID** Honey Grahams, crushed (about 3 tablespoons)
⅔ cup boiling water
1 package (4-serving size) **JELL-O** Orange Flavor Sugar Free Low Calorie Gelatin
1 cup **BREAKSTONE'S** or **KNUDSEN** Low Fat Cottage Cheese
1 container (8 ounces) **PHILADELPHIA** Fat Free Cream Cheese
2 cups thawed **COOL WHIP FREE** Whipped Topping
½ cup chopped fresh pineapple
1 medium kiwi, peeled, sliced

SPRINKLE crumbs onto bottom of 8- or 9-inch springform pan or 9-inch pie plate sprayed with cooking spray.

STIR boiling water into gelatin in large bowl at least 2 minutes until gelatin is completely dissolved. Cool 5 minutes. Pour into blender container. Add cheeses; cover. Blend on medium speed until well blended, occasionally scraping down side of blender container; pour into large bowl. Add whipped topping; stir gently until well blended. Pour into prepared pan; smooth top with spatula.

REFRIGERATE 4 hours or until set. Remove side of pan. Top with fruit just before serving. Store leftover cheesecake in refrigerator.

How To Peel Kiwi: Cut off both ends of the kiwi with a small paring knife. Then, use the knife or a vegetable peeler to remove the fuzzy peel.

Luscious Cream Puffs

Makes 9 servings, I cream puff each.

Total: 45 minutes

- ½ package (17.3 ounces) frozen puff pastry (I sheet), thawed
- I cup milk
- I package (4-serving size) **JELL-O** Vanilla Flavor Instant Pudding & Pie Filling
- ½ cup thawed **COOL WHIP** Whipped Topping
- I square **BAKER'S** Semi-Sweet Baking Chocolate, melted

PREHEAT oven to 400°F. Unfold pastry sheet on lightly floured surface; roll pastry out to 10-inch square. Cut into 9 (3-inch) rounds using cookie cutter or rim of a glass. Place on ungreased baking sheet. Bake 10 minutes; cool completely.

MEANWHILE, pour milk into large bowl. Add dry pudding mix. Beat with wire whisk 2 minutes or until well blended. Gently stir in whipped topping. Cover. Refrigerate 15 minutes.

CUT cream puffs horizontally in half. Spoon pudding mixture evenly into bottom halves of cream puffs; cover with tops. Drizzle with melted chocolate. Serve immediately. Or, cover and refrigerate until ready to serve.

Substitute: Prepare as directed, using **JELL-O** White Chocolate Flavor Instant Pudding & Pie Filling and **COOL WHIP** French Vanilla Whipped Topping.

Triple-Berry Cheesecake Tart

Makes 10 servings, 1 slice each.

Total: 3 hours 30 minutes (includes refrigeration)

1¼ cups finely crushed **NILLA** Wafers (about 45 wafers)
¼ cup (½ stick) butter, melted
1 package (8 ounces) **PHILADELPHIA** Cream Cheese, softened
¼ cup sugar
1 cup thawed **COOL WHIP** Whipped Topping
2 cups mixed berries (raspberries, strawberries and blueberries)
¾ cup boiling water
1 package (4-serving size) **JELL-O** Lemon Flavor Gelatin
1 cup ice cubes

MIX wafer crumbs and butter; press firmly onto bottom and up side of 9-inch tart pan. Place in freezer while preparing filling.

BEAT cream cheese and sugar in large bowl with electric mixer on medium speed until well blended. Gently stir in whipped topping. Spoon into crust. Top with berries. Cover and refrigerate while preparing gelatin.

STIR boiling water into dry gelatin mix in medium bowl 2 minutes until completely dissolved. Add ice cubes; stir until ice is completely melted. Refrigerate 15 minutes or until slightly thickened (consistency of unbeaten egg whites). Spoon gelatin over fruit in pan. Refrigerate 3 hours or until set. Store leftover tart in refrigerator.

Size-Wise: This colorful berry dessert makes a great treat to share with friends and family.

Double Chocolate Mousse

Makes 6 servings, I dessert each.

Total: 30 minutes

1 1/2 cups cold fat free milk, divided
2 squares **BAKER'S** Semi-Sweet Baking Chocolate
1 package (4-serving size) **JELL-O** Chocolate Flavor Fat Free Sugar Free Instant Reduced Calorie Pudding & Pie Filling
2 cups thawed **COOL WHIP FREE** Whipped Topping, divided
1/2 cup fresh raspberries

COMBINE 1 cup of the milk and the chocolate in large microwaveable bowl. Microwave on HIGH 2 minutes; stir until chocolate is completely melted. Stir in remaining 1/2 cup milk. Add dry pudding mix. Beat with wire whisk 2 minutes or until well blended. Refrigerate at least 20 minutes. Gently stir in 1 1/2 cups of the whipped topping.

SPOON into 6 dessert dishes.

TOP with the remaining 1/2 cup whipped topping and the raspberries. Store leftover desserts in refrigerator.

Make Ahead: Prepare as directed, except do not top with the remaining 1/2 cup whipped topping and the raspberries. Refrigerate until ready to serve. Top with the remaining whipped topping and the raspberries just before serving.

Holiday JELL-O JIGGLERS

Makes 2 dozen or 24 servings, 1 **JIGGLERS** each.

Total: 3 hours 10 minutes (includes refrigerating)

2½ cups boiling water (Do not add cold water.)
2 packages (8-serving size each) **JELL-O** Gelatin, any flavor

STIR boiling water into dry gelatin mix in large bowl at least 3 minutes until completely dissolved. Pour into 13×9-inch pan.

REFRIGERATE at least 3 hours or until firm.

DIP bottom of pan in warm water 15 seconds. Cut into 24 decorative shapes using 2-inch cookie cutters, being careful to cut all the way through gelatin to bottom of pan. Lift **JIGGLERS** from pan. Reserve scraps for snacking. Store in tightly covered container in refrigerator.

Make It Easy: Instead of cutting out with cookie cutters, cut the **JELL-O JIGGLERS** into 1-inch cubes.

15 Minute Prep

Holiday Poke Cake

Makes 16 servings, 1 slice each.

Total: 4 hours 15 minutes (includes refrigerating)

- 2   baked (9-inch) round white cake layers, cooled
- 2   cups boiling water
- 1   package (4-serving size) **JELL-O** Gelatin, any red flavor
- 1   package (4-serving size) **JELL-O** Lime Flavor Gelatin
- 1   tub (8 ounces) **COOL WHIP** Whipped Topping, thawed

PLACE cake layers, top sides up, in 2 clean (9-inch) round cake pans. Pierce layers with large fork at ½-inch intervals.

STIR 1 cup of the boiling water into each flavor of dry gelatin mix in separate bowls at least 2 minutes until completely dissolved. Carefully pour red gelatin over 1 cake layer and lime gelatin over second cake layer. Refrigerate 3 hours.

DIP 1 cake pan in warm water 10 seconds; unmold onto serving plate. Spread with about 1 cup of the whipped topping. Unmold second cake layer; carefully place on first cake layer. Frost top and side of cake with remaining whipped topping.

REFRIGERATE at least 1 hour or until ready to serve. Decorate with fresh raspberries, if desired. Store leftover cake in refrigerator.

Special Extra: For an easy, festive touch, sprinkle top of cake with holiday colored sprinkles just before serving.

Seasonal Desserts

Cookies & Cream Snowman Dessert

Makes 10 servings, ½ cup each.

Total: 24 hours 15 minutes (includes refrigerating)

2 cups cold milk
1 package (4-serving size) **JELL-O** Chocolate Flavor Instant Pudding & Pie Filling
30 **OREO** Chocolate Sandwich Cookies, divided
1½ cups thawed **COOL WHIP** Whipped Topping
Decorations: 1 baby carrot and 1 piece black string licorice

POUR milk into medium bowl. Add dry pudding mix. Beat with wire whisk 2 minutes or until well blended.

LINE 8-inch round cake pan with plastic wrap. Arrange 14 of the cookies on bottom of prepared pan; spread 1 cup of the pudding mixture over cookies. Repeat layers of 14 cookies and remaining pudding mixture; cover with plastic wrap.

REFRIGERATE at least 24 hours. Uncover. Invert onto serving plate; remove plastic wrap. Frost with the whipped topping. Add 2 remaining cookies for the eyes and the carrot for the nose. Cut licorice into 6-inch length; add to face for the mouth. Store in refrigerator.

Substitute: Prepare as directed, using **JELL-O** Chocolate Fudge Flavor Instant Pudding & Pie Filling.

Easy Holiday Ribbon Bowl

Makes 8 servings, about ½ cup each.

Total: 2 hours 30 minutes (includes refrigerating)

2¼ cups boiling water, divided
1 package (4-serving size) **JELL-O** Lime Flavor Gelatin
1 cup ice cubes
1 package (4-serving size) **JELL-O** Strawberry Flavor Gelatin
1 tub (8 ounces) **COOL WHIP** Whipped Topping, unthawed, divided

STIR ¾ cup of the boiling water into dry lime gelatin mix in large bowl until completely dissolved. Add ice cubes; stir until slightly thickened. Remove any unmelted ice. Pour into 1- to 1½-quart serving bowl. Refrigerate 15 minutes or until set.

ADD remaining 1½ cups boiling water to dry strawberry gelatin mix in large bowl; stir until gelatin is completely dissolved. Add ⅔ of the frozen whipped topping (about 2 cups); stir with wire whisk until whipped topping is completely melted and mixture is well blended. Refrigerate remaining whipped topping for later use as garnish. Carefully pour strawberry gelatin mixture over lime gelatin layer in bowl.

REFRIGERATE 2 hours or until set. Top with remaining whipped topping just before serving. Store leftover dessert in refrigerator.

Make It Easy: No need to thaw the **COOL WHIP**. By using frozen **COOL WHIP**, the dessert magically layers right before your eyes.

Wave-Your-Flag Cheesecake

Makes 20 servings, about ½ cup each.

Total: 4 hours 25 minutes (includes refrigeration)

1 quart strawberries, divided
1½ cups boiling water
2 packages (4-serving size each) **JELL-O** Strawberry Flavor Gelatin
  Ice cubes
1 cup cold water
1 package (12 ounces) pound cake, cut into 10 slices
1⅓ cups blueberries, divided
2 packages (8 ounces each) **PHILADELPHIA** Cream Cheese, softened
¼ cup sugar
1 tub (8 ounces) **COOL WHIP** Whipped Topping, thawed

SLICE 1 cup of the strawberries; set aside. Halve the remaining 3 cups strawberries; set aside. Stir boiling water into dry gelatin mixes in large bowl at least 2 minutes until completely dissolved. Add enough ice to cold water to measure 2 cups. Add to gelatin; stir until ice is completely melted. Refrigerate 5 minutes or until gelatin is slightly thickened (consistency of unbeaten egg whites).

MEANWHILE, line bottom of 13×9-inch dish with the cake slices. Add sliced strawberries and 1 cup of the blueberries to thickened gelatin; stir gently. Spoon over cake slices. Refrigerate 4 hours or until set.

BEAT cream cheese and sugar in large bowl with wire whisk or electric mixer until well blended; gently stir in whipped topping. Spread over gelatin. Arrange strawberry halves on cream cheese mixture to resemble the stripes of a flag. Arrange the remaining ⅓ cup blueberries on cream cheese mixture for the "stars." Store leftover dessert in refrigerator.

Size-Wise: Enjoy a serving of this easy-to-make dessert on occasion, but keep portion size in mind. One dessert makes enough for 20 servings.

Red, White & Blueberry Parfaits

Makes 8 servings, 1 parfait each.

Total: 4 hours 15 minutes (includes refrigeration)

1 cup boiling water
1 package (4-serving size) **JELL-O** Strawberry
    Flavor Sugar Free Low Calorie Gelatin, or any
    other red flavor
1 cup cold water
1 tub (8 ounces) **COOL WHIP LITE** Whipped
    Topping, thawed, divided
1½ cups blueberries

STIR boiling water into dry gelatin mix in medium bowl at least 2 minutes until completely dissolved. Stir in cold water. Pour into 13×9-inch pan.

REFRIGERATE 4 hours or until firm.

CUT gelatin into ½-inch cubes. Reserve 1 cup of the whipped topping for garnish. Layer blueberries, remaining whipped topping and the gelatin cubes in 8 dessert glasses. Top with the reserved whipped topping. Store in refrigerator.

Nutrition Bonus: Enjoy this low-fat, cholesterol-free treat while sitting in the shade on a hot summer's day! As a bonus, it's also low in sodium!

Substitute: Prepare as directed, using **COOL WHIP** Sugar Free Whipped Topping.

15 Minute Prep

Ghosts in the Graveyard

Makes 18 servings, about ½ cup each.

Total: 1 hour 15 minutes (includes refrigerating)

3 cups cold milk
2 packages (4-serving size each) **JELL-O** Chocolate Flavor Instant Pudding & Pie Filling
1 tub (12 ounces) **COOL WHIP** Whipped Topping, thawed, divided
15 **OREO** Chocolate Sandwich Cookies, crushed
   Assorted decorations: 3 **CAMEO** Creme Sandwich Cookies, decorating gel, 5 candy pumpkins, 10 pieces of candy corn

POUR milk into large bowl. Add dry pudding mixes. Beat with wire whisk 2 minutes or until well blended. Let stand 5 minutes. Gently stir in 3 cups of the whipped topping and half of the cookie crumbs. Spread evenly into 13×9-inch baking dish; sprinkle with the remaining cookie crumbs.

REFRIGERATE at least 1 hour. Meanwhile, decorate creme sandwich cookies with decorating gel to resemble tombstones. Set aside until ready to use.

INSERT decorated cookies into top of dessert just before serving. Add candies. Drop large spoonfuls of the remaining whipped topping onto dessert to resemble ghosts. Cover and store leftover dessert in refrigerator.

How To Make Green Grass: Use snipped pieces of green chewy fruit snack rolls to create "grass" around the graveyard.

Boo Cups

Makes 15 servings, one Boo Cup each.

Total: 15 minutes

3¼ cups cold milk

2 packages (4-serving size each) **JELL-O** Chocolate Flavor Instant Pudding & Pie Filling

1 tub (8 ounces) **COOL WHIP** Whipped Topping, thawed, divided

20 **OREO** Chocolate Sandwich Cookies, crushed, divided

30 miniature semi-sweet chocolate chips

POUR milk into large bowl. Add dry pudding mixes. Beat with wire whisk 2 minutes or until well blended. Gently stir in half each of the whipped topping and cookie crumbs.

SPOON 1 tablespoon of the remaining cookie crumbs into each of 15 (6-ounce) paper or plastic cups. Cover evenly with layers of the pudding mixture and remaining cookie crumbs.

DROP remaining whipped topping by spoonfuls onto desserts to resemble ghosts. Add chocolate chips for the eyes. Serve immediately. Or, refrigerate until ready to serve. Cover and store leftover desserts in refrigerator.

Shortcut: Instead of dropping spoonfuls of whipped topping, use a resealable plastic bag to make the ghosts. Fill bag with remaining whipped topping; seal bag. Using scissors, diagonally snip off one corner from bottom of bag. Squeeze out topping to resemble the ghosts.